Ripley Readers

Bears!

All true and unbelievable!

PUBLISHING

a Jim Pattison Company

Big claws! Big teeth!
What can it be?

It is a bear!

Bears have black, brown,
or white fur.

Look, this one has two colors!

Bears like honey, but they eat bugs, fish, and grass, too!

Wow!

A bear can run
as fast as a horse!

This bear wants to jump
in the water.

Did you know many bears
are good swimmers?

You can find bears all over
the world!

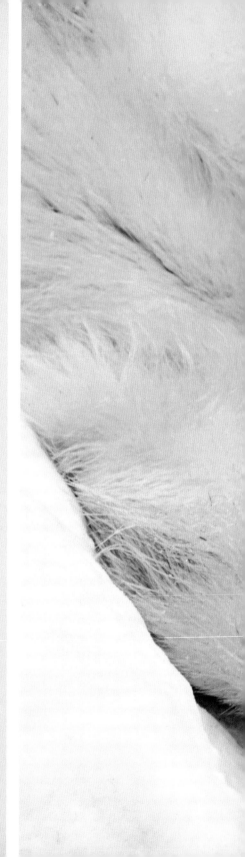

There are eight kinds of bears.

How many can you name?

Not all bears go to sleep
in the winter.

Pandas have a lot to eat all year!

A panda can eat 20 pounds of bamboo a day!

Polar bears are the biggest.
They can stand almost as tall
as a basketball hoop!

Look out, fish!

That polar bear can swim faster than the fastest human can!

Sun bears are little, but they are good at climbing up trees!

Did you know some black bears are white?

They are called spirit bears.

Sloth bears look funny with no front teeth!

 30

These animals are bear-y cool!

Ripley Readers

Ready for More?

Ripley Readers feature unbelievable but true facts and stories!

LEVEL ONE — Sounding it out

LEVEL TWO — Reading with help

LEVEL THREE — Independent reading

LEVEL FOUR — Chapters

For more information about Ripley's Believe It or Not!, go to www.ripleys.com